TOP CLASS

Vocabulary

Year 4

Now supported with CPD training
For info visit www.johnmurraycpd.co.uk

John Murray

Published by Hopscotch, a division of
MA Education, St Jude's Church,
Dulwich Road, London, SE24 0PB
www.hopscotchbooks.com
020 7738 5454

©2016 MA Education Ltd

Written by John Murray

Series designed by Claire Swaffield,
Fonthill Creative, 01722 717029

Cover illustration by Sara Anderton
www.catandfoxadventures.com

Illustrations by Emma Turner and Sara Anderton
Page 9 photograph: Lewis Carroll [Public domain],
via Wikimedia Commons

Associate Publisher: Angela Morano Shaw

ISBN 978 1909 860148

All rights reserved. This resource is sold subject to the condition that it shall not, by way of trade or otherwise, be lent, hired out or otherwise circulated without the publisher's prior consent in any form of binding or cover other than that in which it is published and without a similar condition, including this condition, being imposed upon the subsequent purchaser.

No part of this publication may be reproduced, stored in a retrieval system, or transmitted, in any form or by any means, electronic, mechanical, photocopying, recording or otherwise, without the prior permission of the publisher, except where photocopying for educational purposes within the school or other educational establishment that has purchased this book is expressly permitted in the text.

Every effort has been made to trace the owners of copyright of material in this book and the publisher apologises for any inadvertent omissions. Any persons claiming copyright for any material should contact the publisher who will be happy to pay the permission fees agreed between them and who will amend the information in this book on any subsequent reprint.

Contents Page

Introduction	6
Word Meaning I	8
Word Meaning II	12
Word Families I	16
Word Families II	20
Prefixes	24
Suffixes	28
Compound Words	32
Synonyms	36
Homophones	40
Homonyms	44
Formal English	48
Informal Speech	52
Similes	56
Creative Word Play	60

Introduction

Top Class is a series that endeavours to combine traditional approaches to the teaching and learning of grammar, punctuation and vocabulary with new techniques and activities that support and encourage good learning.

The three core areas have been separated into three distinct books aimed primarily at Key Stage 2. The three books ought to be used in conjunction with each other in order to provide learners with a wider learning environment and for them to understand that these core elements of Literacy work together and are not to be applied in isolation.

Specific elements of the new Key Stage 3 National Curriculum have also been included in order to introduce Key Stage 2 learners to more complex grammatical constructions and vocabulary as they make their transition from attaining National Standard to Mastery in writing.

Each book, one for each Year group in Key Stage 2, aims to promote discussion about specific areas of Literacy and provide experiences and opportunities to use and apply what they have learnt.

The three books are as follows:

- **Top Class – Grammar**
- **Top Class – Punctuation**
- **Top Class – Vocabulary**

Each book contains lessons that develop a 'top-down' approach, allowing learners to see how we use language in context, not simply *when* we use a particular word, punctuation mark or grammatical construct but *how* to use it to its best effect when writing independently.

As such, it actively promotes the core principle that to learn grammar and punctuation well and to extend your personal vocabulary effectively, then you must not only see these particular elements of Literacy within authentic and meaningful context and settings but you must then have the opportunity to apply what you have understood in your own independent writing.

All too often children are taught grammar, punctuation and vocabulary with exercises that aren't rooted within an authentic experience; and, as a result, although they may gain full marks in their exercise books, they often misapply or omit what has been learnt in their own free writing.

The *Top Class* series seeks to address this problem using a three staged approach, each Lesson Plan being structured so that learners are encouraged to investigate and explore the English language; initially with support and guidance from their teacher and fellow peers before being asked to apply what they have learnt as individuals.

Think about...

Before undertaking the Guided activity, learners are asked about what they already know about a particular piece of punctuation or grammatical form and where they might have seen it.

This links directly to the Guided text, again helping learners to view grammar, punctuation and vocabulary in context, housing it so that stronger links can be made with prior learning and personal experiences. This can then be used as a springboard to explore and develop this further in a familiar setting.

For example, when looking at our use of capital letters when writing a proper noun, learners may be asked about why people use an atlas or map before looking at a tourist map of London and considering why place names and famous tourist attractions start with a capital letter.

Guided

This is a shared activity that engages the whole class.

Set within a specific and relevant genre of Literacy, it embeds each particular piece of grammar, punctuation or vocabulary being taught in a focused and meaningful way. Moreover, it invites learners to use this information in order to answer a series of questions that are related to the text itself and then begins to move beyond it.

Each of the three questions asked have been carefully formatted so that valuable practice for the end of *Key Stage 2 English grammar, punctuation and spelling test* can be undertaken throughout each Year group. Marks are also available so that pupils gain practice at providing fuller explanations for those questions where two or three marks are being awarded. Answers are provided on the Lesson Plan.

Independent

This activity can be completed as an individual, with a partner or within a small group.

Each Independent activity within the book is also differentiated at an upper and lower level* and offers teachers a range of practical activities that support learners as they practice what they have learnt in the Guided section.

*Differentiated activities can be found on the CD Rom.

Homework

Included in this section is a homework activity that aims to encourage wider learning outside of the classroom to take place. There are two types of homework activities that are provided, each having been designed to help learners discover and engage with grammar, punctuation and vocabulary in the 'real' world:

A] Specific 'closed' questions may be asked in order that research skills, both modern and traditional, can be employed to find a particular answer.

For example: What is the capital city of Denmark? Who was the first man to walk on the moon? When necessary, answers are provided on the Lesson Plan.

B] Wider 'open' tasks are given in order to afford learners the opportunity to explore the world around them and collect examples that are both pertinent and authentic.

For example, learners may be asked to find three examples where a shop's name uses an apostrophe in their local high street.

Extension

This final stage of the learning journey is an important one and underscores the importance of using a 'top-down' approach to the teaching and learning of grammar, punctuation and vocabulary.

Each Extension activity within the book is also differentiated at an upper and lower level.*

Its aim is to encourage children to apply what they have learnt in a meaningful and purposeful way in order to embed their learning.

For example, learners may be asked to write a shopping list when planning a party that will naturally include a colon or use strong adjectives to describe a certain event in a story.

More importantly, it is this *writing for purpose* (rather than to score arbitrary marks or achieve irrelevant ticks in an exercise book) that provides a meaningful opportunity for individuals to engage with the English language and create their own work that uses grammar, punctuation and vocabulary in a way that brings their work to life.

In this way, not only will each learner be encouraged to use particular forms of grammar, punctuation or vocabulary correctly but, essentially, they will gain a strong sense of themselves taking an active role as a writer. It gives them a valuable sense of what it is like to be an author, one who uses grammar not only to improve the quality of their work but also to express themselves as best they can using the written word.

The journey from simply understanding how the English language works to being able to apply that knowledge in order to become a capable and confident writer is a journey that will continue into adulthood and one that, in all truthfulness, never really ends.

However, by providing meaningful activities for both the classroom and beyond, the *Top Class* series can help each and every writer to freely use grammar, punctuation and vocabulary to great effect and support them as they endeavour to bring the written word to life in order to inform, influence and entertain their readers.

Differentiated activities can be found on the CD Rom.

Word Meaning I

Think about...
What do you do if you see an unknown word?
How do you work it out?
"She grabbed a pen and began _____ down her ideas."
What might the missing word be?
Why do you think this?

Guided

A virus has attacked your computer.

What is a computer virus? How might this affect your computer? Have you heard the word 'virus' before? Where? When? Why do you think a word associated with people becoming ill has been adopted for something that attacks and infects a computer?

Once done, answer the questions on page 9.

Independent

The same virus has attacked your laptop. Be a reading detective and restore your homework.

On your own, with a partner or in a small group; complete the task sheet provided to you by your teacher on page 10.

Once finished, cut off the homework task to help you broaden your word knowledge through practical reading within a variety of contexts.

Extension

Extend your personal vocabulary and understanding of specific words. Complete the task sheet on page 11.

If you have one, put any words you find interesting in your Personal Dictionary, together with an example of how it can be used effectively in a sentence.

* Answers available on the CD Rom.

Answers

1 The words, in the correct order, are as follows: heralds, dappled, enthralled, manuscript, auction, equivalent.

2 Allow for personal response.

3a cloudless

3b hopeful/hopeless, careful/careless, helpful/helpless

Homework

- Charles Lutwidge Dodgson
- 26th November, 1865
- Alice's Adventures Under Ground
- Through the Looking Glass

Remember...
When we come across a word we don't know, we can sometimes work out what it means by using clues in the rest of the text. It's like being a **reading detective**...the more **clues** we find, the more likely we are to work out what this new word means.

Word Meaning I

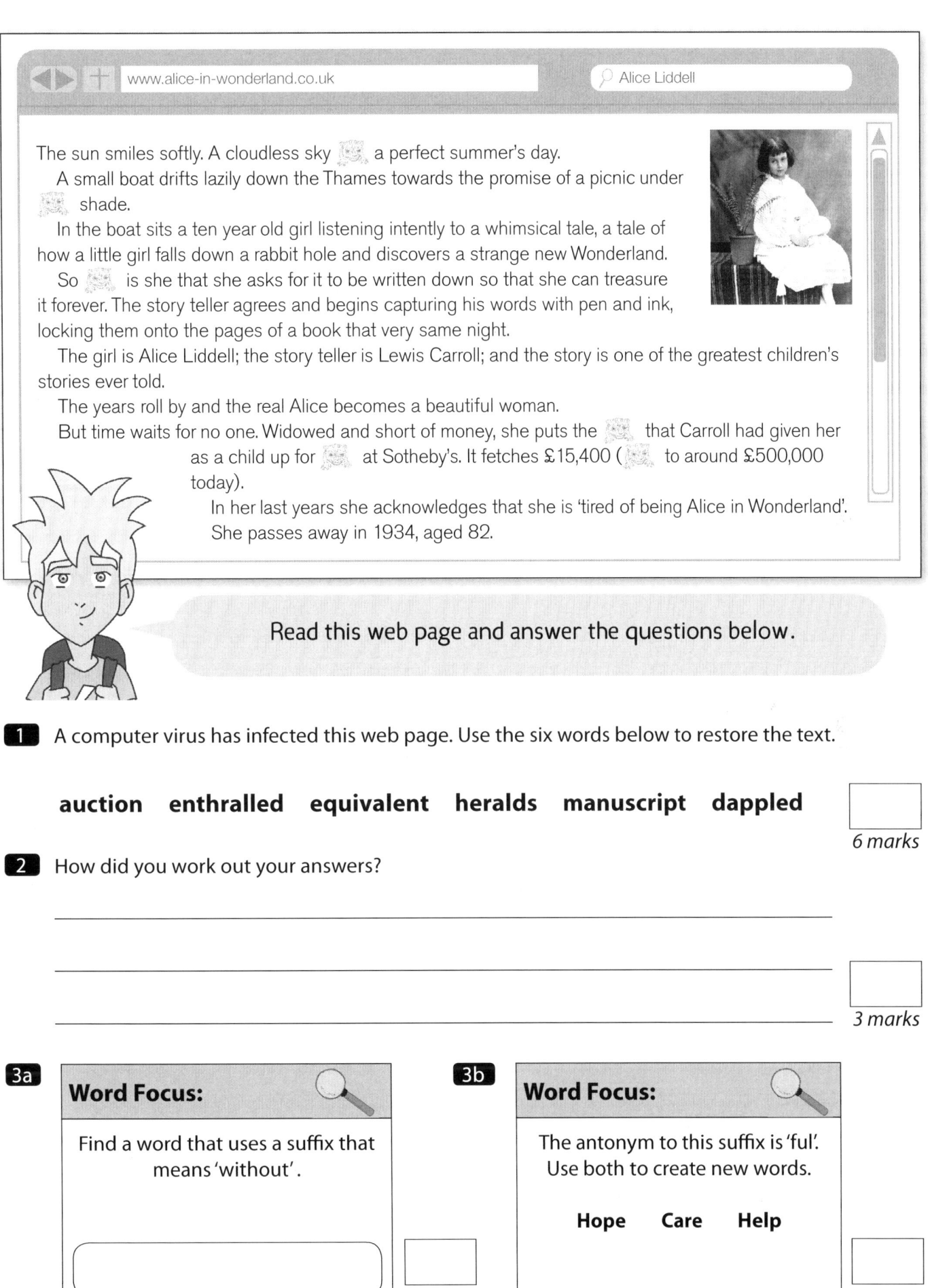

1 A computer virus has infected this web page. Use the six words below to restore the text.

auction   enthralled   equivalent   heralds   manuscript   dappled

6 marks

2 How did you work out your answers?

_____

_____

3 marks

3a Word Focus:

Find a word that uses a suffix that means 'without'.

1 mark

3b Word Focus:

The antonym to this suffix is 'ful'. Use both to create new words.

Hope   Care   Help

3 marks

TOP CLASS - Vocabulary - Year 4

Word Meaning I

A virus has attacked your computer.
Use the clues to work out what each word is meant to be.
Draw and label your answer.
Colour the clues that helped you green.

The Virus!

I couldn't ride my bike because it had a 🦠.

"Call the 🦠," she yelled. "There's been a murder!"

I love 🦠 food. Spaghetti Bolognese is my favourite.

You'll need an 🦠, it's pouring down outside.

Turn the 🦠 down! Can't you see I'm on the phone?

Clickety clack, clickety clack, the 🦠 train sped down the railway track.

"It's 🦠 in here," said Jacob taking off his jumper.

I'd rather have 🦠 on my toast than margarine.

Homework

Read about *Alice's Adventures in Wonderland*.
* What was Lewis Carroll's real name?
* In what year was this book first published?
* What was the original title of the book?
* What is the sequel to this book?

Vocabulary

Revisit the text on page 9. Answer each question below.
Highlight the words you explore in the text itself.
Think of ways in which you can learn each one.
Can you act it out or draw it?
Does it remind you of a word you already know? Why?
How will you use your new words in the future?

Name: **Date:**

Describe a person that has been '**widowed**'.
- [ ] They have never been married
- [ ] They are divorced
- [ ] Their husband or wife has died
- [ ] They are single

What is a polite way of saying a person has died?

What does it mean to be '**short of money**'?
- [ ] You have lots of money to spend
- [ ] You have just enough money to spend
- [ ] You do not have enough money to spend

What does the word '**tired**' mean in paragraph eight?
- [ ] In need of a rest or sleep
- [ ] Bored, no longer finds it interesting
- [ ] Looks old and worn out

Underline the root in the word

acknowledges

Can you spot another family word?

If you '**treasure**' a book, how much do you like it?

A little   A lot

1   2   3   4   5

Why?

If you are '**enthralled**' by something, how interesting do you find it?

Not very interesting   Very interesting

1   2   3   4   5

Why?

What do we call a copy of a book before it goes to press?

Is this version usually typed up or handwritten?

Word Meaning II

Think about...
You come across an unfamiliar word.
What do you do next?
"Gran placed her _____ teeth in the glass."
What might the missing word be?
Why do you think this?

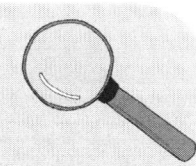

Guided

The computer virus has struck again! This time it has deleted Key Words.

How might you work out what each of the missing words might be? How can you check if the word you have chosen is correct? Why might somebody else have chosen a different word to you and both be correct?

Once done, answer the questions on page 13.

Independent

Be a Reading Detective and work out the missing words.

On your own, with a partner or in a small group; complete the task sheet provided to you by your teacher on page 14.

Once finished, cut off the homework task to help you broaden your word knowledge through practical reading within a variety of contexts.

Extension

Extend your personal vocabulary and understanding of specific words. Complete the task sheet on page 15.

If you have one, put any words you find interesting in your Personal Dictionary, together with an example of how it can be used effectively in a sentence.

*Answers available on the CD Rom.

Answers

1 The words, in the correct order, are as follows: entire, emerge, permanent, unique, assisting, average.

2 Allow for personal response.

3a unique

3b Allow for personal definitions to be made but compare with those found in a class or online dictionary.

Homework

- 32 (just like us humans)

- 60 (at any one time). They grow between 2000-3000 in a lifetime.

- Elephants - their tusks are actually teeth!

- Dolphins – they can have up to 200!

Remember...
When we come across a word we don't know, we can sometimes work it out by using clues in the rest of the text. It's like being a **reading detective**...the more **clues** we find, the more likely we are to work out what this new word might be.

Word Meaning II

www.funfacts.co.uk/teeth | Teeth

Fun Facts To Sink Your Teeth Into

1. The enamel on the top surface on your tooth is the hardest part of your _____ body.
2. Teeth start to form even before you are born. Your milk teeth start to form when you are in the womb but only _____ when you are between 6-12 months old.
3. Ancient tribes of Mexico would replace lost or damaged teeth with the teeth of animals, such as wolves or other wild beasts.
4. False teeth not included, humans have only two sets of teeth in their lifetime: 20 milk (or baby) teeth and 32 _____ teeth.
5. No two people have the same set of teeth. Your teeth are as _____ as you, so be proud of your pearly whites.
6. Your mouth produces between 2-4 pints of spit per day; that's enough to fill two swimming pools in a lifetime. Saliva has many uses, including _____ you with your digestion and protecting your teeth from bacteria and decay in your mouth.
7. The _____ person spends 38.5 days brushing their teeth over their lifetime.
8. If you get your tooth knocked out, put it in milk - this helps the tooth to survive longer while you make your way to the dentist.

Look at this Fact File and answer the questions below.

1 Use the six words below to reverse the computer virus.

permanent   assisting   entire   average   unique   emerge

6 marks

2 How did you work out your answers?

_____

_____

_____

3 marks

3a Word Focus:
Which of these missing words uses a prefix that means 'one'?

1 mark

3b Word Focus:
Why do you think these words use the same prefix?

uniform   unicycle   unicorn

3 marks

TOP CLASS - Vocabulary - Year 4

Word Meaning II

The computer virus has returned. Read each sentence. Use the clues to work out what each word is meant to be. Draw and label your answer.
Colour the clues that helped you blue.

The Virus Returns!

🦠 sugars, please. I'm afraid I have a sweet tooth.

We'd better call an 🦠. This looks pretty serious.

My 🦠 is in the wash? The match is tonight!

The stars were out. An 🦠 hooted in the darkness beyond.

I'm 🦠. I could eat a scabby donkey!

Button up your coat. It's 🦠 outside.

Sailing the 🦠 into the harbour was easy now that the storm was over.

I'm 🦠! I haven't drunken anything all day.

- ✂

Homework

Read about teeth in the animal kingdom.
- How many teeth do giraffes have?
- How many teeth do crocodiles have?
- Which animal has the longest teeth?
- Which animal has the most teeth at one time?

Vocabulary

Revisit the text on page 13. Answer each question below.
Highlight the words you explore in the text itself.
Think of ways in which you can learn each one.
Can you act it out or draw it?
Does it remind you of a word you already know? Why?
How will you use your new words in the future?

Name: **Date:**

What is the scientific word for '**spit**'?

What is the '**average**' of the following numbers?

3   10   9   7   11

Show your working out.

Find a word that means
'**lasting for a long time or forever**'.

Why do some marker pens use this adjective?

If something is '**unique**' how many copies are there?

1   2   3   4   5   6   7   8   9   10

How many more '**uni**' words can you think of?

Find a formal word for '**keeping safe**'.

Put this word in a sentence of your own.

Find a formal word for '**helping**'.

Put this word in a sentence of your own.

Which hard material covers the top surface of a tooth?

Find a word that means '**very old**'?

Put this word in a sentence of your own.

TOP CLASS - Vocabulary - Year 4

Word Families I

Think about...
Look at the following words:
horror joking October horrible joker octagon joke octopus horrendous
Match the words that relate to each other.
Circle the root.

Guided

You are researching the origins of Trick-or-Treating.

What time of year do you associate with this custom? What else do you associate with this custom? From which country do you think it comes? Why might some people not like this custom? Do you think it is something that children should participate in? Why? Why not? Make a list for and against Trick-or-Treating with your teacher.

Once done, answer the questions on page 17.

Independent

Consider the origins of names.

On your own, with a partner or in a small group; complete the task sheet provided to you by your teacher on page 18.

Once finished, cut off the homework task to help you broaden your word knowledge through practical reading within a variety of contexts.

Extension

Extend your personal vocabulary and understanding of specific words. Complete the task sheet on page 19.

If you have one, put any words you find interesting in your Personal Dictionary, together with an example of how it can be used effectively in a sentence.

*Answers available on the CD Rom.

Answers

1 original/originates, ghoul/ghoulish, disguise/guising, migrant/immigrants

2 Allow for personal response.

3a October

This is the tenth month due to the introduction of two extra months named after Roman Caesars:
Julius (July) in 44 BC
Augustus (August) in 8 BC.

3b Allow for personal response.

Homework

- No specific answers are required for this homework. Teachers should allow learners to make personal choices as to the celebration (religious, cultural or otherwise) they wish to present. This will not only help individuals take ownership of the presentation itself but also better reflect the diversity of beliefs and practices represented within any given class.

Remember...
When we understand the **root** of a word, then we can begin to understand how different words that use the same root relate to each other. Learning **word families** is a great way to extend your word knowledge and appreciate where words come from.

Word Families I

TRICK OR TREAT

Dating back some two thousand years, Halloween originates from the ancient Celtic festival of *Samhain*, later celebrated as *All Saint's Day* on November 1st.

It was believed that on the night before (October 31st) the dead would return as ghosts and so people would leave food, wine and other treats on their doorsteps to keep the evil spirits at bay.

And if any were brave enough to leave the house on this ghoulish night, they would be sure to wear a mask in the hope of going unnoticed by the spirits that roamed the streets.

By the 8th century this had grown into the tradition of *Guising* where children would be sent out in costume to accept food, wine and money in exchange for singing a song, reciting a poem or telling a joke.

Fast forward to 19th century America and we see Scottish and Irish immigrants reviving this macabre tradition to help remind them of times back home. The result…the *Trick-or-Treat* spectacle we still see to this day.

Read this article and answer the questions below.

1 Find the word that is most likely to be related to the following:

original [ ]   ghoul [ ]   disguise [ ]   migrant [ ]

4 marks

2 How do you think each word is related?

_____

_____

_____

4 marks

3a Word Focus:
Which month begins with a prefix that means 'eight'?

1 mark

3b Word Focus:
List three more words that use this same prefix for the same reason.

3 marks

Word Families 1

Match each month with how it got its name.
Use a different colour for each month.
Which months are named after gods?
Which months are named after people?
Which months are named after numbers?

Our Calendar:

January	February	March	April	May	June

This month gains its name from *Maia*, the Roman goddess of growing plants.	The Latin word *octo* means eight.		The Roman festival *Februa* celebrated the end of the Roman calendar.		This month's name comes from the queen of the Roman gods, *Juno*, who looked over marriages and weddings.
The Latin word *septum* means seven.	Named after the Roman god for beginnings and endings *Janus*.		*Decem* is Latin for ten.		All wars stopped during the Roman New Year, hence the link to *Mars* the Roman god of war.
Named after Caesar *Augustus* in 8 BC.	Some claim this month comes from *aperire*, a Latin word meaning 'to open', referring to how flowers open in spring.		From the Latin word *novem*, meaning nine.		*Julius* Caesar gave his name to this month in 44 BC.

July	August	September	October	November	December

Homework
Research a day that is special to you. Why is it so special? Where does it come from? How do you celebrate it? When? Do you wear any special clothes or eat special food during this time? Who are you likely to celebrate this day with?

Vocabulary

Revisit the text on page 17. Answer each question below. Highlight the words you explore in the text itself. Think of ways in which you can learn each one. Can you act it out or draw it? Does it remind you of a word you already know? Why? How will you use your new words in the future?

Name: **Date:**

Which synonym does the writer use instead of **'wicked'**?

Use this word in a sentence of your own.

What do we call people who come from the following lands?

Scotland: _____

Ireland: _____

In paragraph one, which adjective is used to describe people linked with Scotland and Ireland?

Which people of the UK can also use this word?

In paragraph four, which formal word means **'reading a story or poem out loud from memory'**?

Underline a synonym for **'ghost'** in the word

ghoulish

Check your answer in a dictionary.

In paragraph three, which word means **'not seen'**?

Is this word more likely to be positive or negative?

(+)   (-)

Who is an **'immigrant'**?

☐ Somebody who enters a country to look for work

☐ Somebody who leaves a country to look for work

In the final paragraph, which word means **'bringing back to life'**?

TOP CLASS - Vocabulary - Year 4

Word Families II

Think about...
Look at the following words: **electric television chemical telescope electrician chemist telephone electrical chemistry**
Match the words that relate to each other. Circle the root. How are they related?

Guided

You are walking past a billboard poster.

Who do you think Billy Whizz is? Do you think he is a good or a bad wizard? Why do you think this? How entertaining do you think his act would be? What sorts of illusions and tricks might you see? Would you be tempted to go and watch such a show? Why? Why not?

Once done, answer the questions on page 21.

Independent

Consider the root meaning of different words.

On your own, with a partner or in a small group; complete the task sheet provided to you by your teacher on page 22.

Once finished, cut off the homework task to help you broaden your word knowledge through practical reading within a variety of contexts.

Extension

Extend your personal vocabulary and understanding of specific words. Complete the task sheet on page 23.

If you have one, put any words you find interesting in your Personal Dictionary, together with an example of how it can be used effectively in a sentence.

*Answers available on the CD Rom.

Answers

1 magic/magical, illusion/illusionist, spectator/spectacular, busy/business

2 Allow for personal response.

3a **O**ld **A**ge **P**ensioner

3b **W** – William Warlock, wonderful wizardry to wow
C – a clever bit of conjuring, creating chaos
M – Mischief and mayhem are my middle, magical Monday
D – dazzling displays to delight
T – tantalising trickery to tease
P – perfectly precise
S – Spectacular spells

Homework

- July 31st – the same as JK Rowling!
- Harry Potter and the Philosopher's Stone
- Lord Voldemort
- Ron Weasley, Hermione Granger

Remember...
When we understand the root of a word, then we can begin to understand how different words that use the same **root** relate to each other. Learning **word families** is a great way to extend your word knowledge and appreciate where words come from.

Word Families II

Billy Whizz

Mischief and mayhem are my middle names. Well, actually they're Cuthbert and Archibald but where's the alliteration in that? William Warlock is my stage name of course but you can call me Billy Whizz. Everyone else does!
And why have I endured such a long and prosperous career?
Well I suppose it's because I love my job.
Oh you can't beat a clever bit of conjuring you know, creating chaos wherever I go. The greatest illusionist in the business!
Spectacular spells to feast your eyes upon, dazzling displays to delight one and all and tantalising trickery to tease your imagination.
Wonderful wizardry to wow the crowds!
So why not join me this magical Monday
(at 19:31pm to be perfectly precise)
and enjoy a night you will never forget.

Adults: £10 Children (under 12 yrs): £5
Family Ticket: £25 (2 adults & 2 children) OAPs: £7.50

Look at this advertisement and answer the questions below.

1 Find the word that is most likely to be related to the following:

magic ☐   illusion ☐   spectator ☐   busy ☐

4 marks

2 How do you think each word is related?

_____

_____

4 marks

3a Word Focus:
What does the acronym 'OAP' stand for?

1 mark

3b Word Focus:
Make a list of the alliteration using the following letters:

W C M D T P S

3 marks

TOP CLASS - Vocabulary - Year 4

Word Families II

We shorten a person's name when we know them very well. It is warm and friendly. We use our full name when it is an important form or event. Fill in the table below. Underline the root in each name.
On what occasion might you use each form?

Family & Friends!

Formal	Occasion	Informal	Occasion
<u>Ben</u>jamin	Wedding invitation	Ben	Text message
		Sam	Phone call from sister
Alexander	Birth Certificate		
	Letter from bank	Mike	
Joshua			BBQ party
Elizabeth			Birthday card
	When being told off	Danny	
	Parking fine	Charlie	
Victoria			Email from a friend
	School report	Nicky	
Andrew	Signing a cheque		
		Bob	Get well soon card
	Class register	Chris	

Homework

Read about the boy wizard *Harry Potter*.
- When is Harry's birthday?
- In which book did he first appear?
- Who is his arch enemy?
- Who are his two best friends?

Vocabulary

Revisit the text on page 21. Answer each question below.
Highlight the words you explore in the text itself.
Think of ways in which you can learn each one.
Can you act it out or draw it?
Does it remind you of a word you already know? Why?
How will you use your new words in the future?

Name: **Date:**

Find another word we use instead of '**wizard**'.

_____

Is this word usually positive or negative?

(+)   (−)

In line five, which word tells us this wizard is successful and makes a lot of money?

What is the name of this wizard?

Formal: _____

Informal: _____

How else might we shorten his name?

List the two synonyms in line nine that mean '**very exciting to watch**'.

Find a synonym for the word '**mayhem**'.

What do both of these words mean?

What do we call an entertainer who performs tricks where objects appear and disappear?

How naughty is somebody who causes '**mischief**'?

Not naughty   *Very naughty*

(1   2   3   4   5)

How do you think the word '**mischievous**' is related?

What word means '**exact**' or '**accurate**'?

Check your answer in a dictionary.

TOP CLASS - Vocabulary - Year 4

Prefixes

Think about...
Look at the following words:
known allowed spell sense perfect understood mature polite honest stop
Are these words positive or negative?
Add a prefix to each word to make its antonym.

Guided

Your teacher will show you a picture of a tiger.

What do you think of when you see this creature? Write down your thoughts on a wipe board. Wander around your classroom like a stealthy tiger. Your teacher will bang a drum. Stop and growl at the person next to you. Share your ideas with your fellow tiger. Do this three times. Share your favourite thought with the rest of the class. Your teacher will now read a famous poem that describes a tiger. Are any of your ideas included?

Once done, answer the questions on page 25.

Independent

You are investigating how to turn positive words into their negative form.

On your own, with a partner or in a small group; complete the task sheet provided to you by your teacher on page 26.

Once finished, cut off the homework task to help you broaden your word knowledge through practical reading within a variety of contexts.

Extension

Extend your personal vocabulary and understanding of specific words. Complete the task sheet on page 27.

If you have one, put any words you find interesting in your Personal Dictionary, together with an example of how it can be used effectively in a sentence.

*Answers available on the CD Rom.

Answers

1 immortal – to live for ever

2 impossible, disagree, illegal, non fiction, unwrap, misbehave

3a Allow for personal response.

3b thine, thy, thee

Homework

- Six: Amur, Bengal, Indochinese, Malayan, South China, Sumatran

- Three: Balinese, Caspian, Javan

- A tigon or liger

- An ambush or streak

Remember...
A prefix is found at the start of a word. We use many different prefixes such as 'un', 'dis', 'im', 'non' and 'mis' to turn a positive word into its negative form.

Prefixes

The Tyger
BY WILLIAM BLAKE

Tyger Tyger, burning bright,
In the forests of the night;
What immortal hand or eye,
Could frame thy fearful symmetry?

In what distant deeps or skies.
Burnt the fire of thine eyes?
On what wings dare he aspire?
What the hand, dare seize the fire?

And what shoulder, & what art,
Could twist the sinews of thy heart?
And when thy heart began to beat,
What dread hand? & what dread feet?

What the hammer? What the chain,
In what furnace was thy brain?
What the anvil? What dread grasp,
Dare its deadly terrors clasp!

When the stars threw down their spears
And water'd heaven with their tears:
Did he smile his work to see?
Did he who made the Lamb make thee?

Tyger Tyger burning bright,
In the forests of the night:
What immortal hand or eye,
Dare frame thy fearful symmetry?

Look at this classic poem and answer the questions below.

1 Find a word that uses the prefix 'im'. What does this word mean?

2 marks

2 Add prefixes to the following words to change them from positive to negative.

possible   **agree**   **legal**

correct   **wrap**   **behave**

3 marks

3a Word Focus:
How is 'tiger' spelt in this poem? Why?

1 mark

3b Word Focus:
List three words that suggest this poem is very old.

3 marks

TOP CLASS - Vocabulary - Year 4

Prefixes

Look at the words below. Place each one in a ring. Which prefix did you add? Why?
Is your new word positive or negative?
Can any words use more than one prefix?
Choose two words from each ring.
Put it in a sentence of your own.

Why are you being so negative?

kind
reversible
understand
honest
possible
known
cover
logical
like
able
clean
print

un
dis
mis
im
ir
il
-

legal
regular
mature
perfect
lock
tidy
appear
spell
allowed
polite

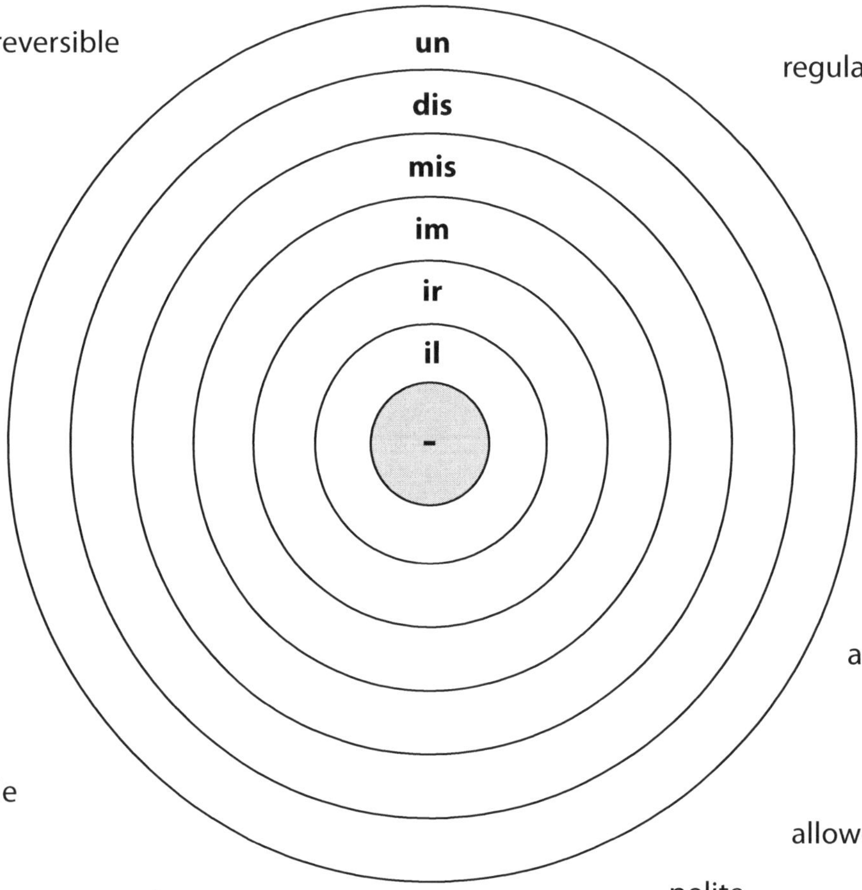

Homework

Read about tigers.
- How many species of tigers are there?
- How many species of tigers are extinct?
- What do we call a cub that is half tiger, half lion?
- What do we call a group of tigers?

Vocabulary

Revisit the text on page 25. Answer each question below. Highlight the words you explore in the text itself. Think of ways in which you can learn each one. Can you act it out or draw it? Does it remind you of a word you already know? Why? How will you use your new words in the future?

Name:	Date:
Find a word that means '**full of fear**'.	Find a word that means '**to live forever**'.
Can you think of another word that uses this same suffix?	What is its antonym?
Find two words that mean '**to grab quickly, with force**'.	Which Old English word means '**you**'? **thine thy thee**
	What do you think the other two words mean?
How worried are you if you are full of '**dread**'? *A little worried* — *Extremely worried* 1 2 3 4 5 Is this word positive or negative? (+) (−)	What scientific name do we give to '**strong tissues that connect muscle to bone**'?
	Check your answer in a dictionary.
What do we call '**a special oven that can be heated up so hot, it causes metal to soften and melt**'?	Draw and label an '**anvil**'.
Draw and label your answer.	Who would use an anvil? Why?

TOP CLASS - Vocabulary - Year 4

Suffixes

Think about...
Look at the following words:
cold warm windy sunny bad wet hot large late beautiful
Add 'er' or 'est' to each word.
What rules do you notice?

Guided

You are reading the reminiscence of the writer's grandfather.

Do you think it is important to have a good relationship with your grandparents? Why? Close your eyes. Is there a special time that you can remember spending with your grandparents? Why was it so special? Why do you treasure this memory? Do you think it is important to talk about the good times we had with family and friends, even when they may no longer be with us? Why?

Once done, answer the questions on page 29.

Independent

You are investigating comparatives and superlatives.

On your own, with a partner or in a small group; complete the task sheet provided to you by your teacher on page 30.

Once finished, cut off the homework task to help you broaden your word knowledge through practical reading within a variety of contexts.

Extension

Extend your personal vocabulary and understanding of specific words. Complete the task sheet on page 31.

If you have one, put any words you find interesting in your Personal Dictionary, together with an example of how it can be used effectively in a sentence.

*Answers available on the CD Rom.

Answers

1 kind – kinder – kindest
warm – warmer – warmest

2 tall – taller – tallest
soft – softer – softest
brave – braver – bravest
large – larger – largest
thin – thinner – thinnest
wet – wetter – wettest
lazy – lazier – laziest
lucky – luckier – luckiest

3a extraordinary
(extra / ordinary)

3b good – better – best (irregular)

Homework

- No specific answers are required for this homework. However, teachers should be aware that some learners will choose to describe a loved one that is no longer with us. Sensitivity must therefore be given when both setting this task and when deciding upon how learners are to present their work.

Remember...
A suffix is found at the end of a word. When we add '**er**' to some words we turn it into a **comparative** word and when we add '**est**' we turn it into a **superlative** word. If the word has three syllables or more, we use '**more**' for comparatives and '**most**' for superlatives.

Suffixes

This is my granddad, Reginald Jones.
He was a good man, a man of great stature both in height and of heart. He was not famous. Nor was he rich. He lived an ordinary life; worked in an ordinary job and lived in an ordinary council house in an ordinary town.
If it wasn't for me writing this, you would never have seen his kind face or his warm smile. If I hadn't written this then you would never have been able to put a name to that kind face or warm smile.
But I have put pen to paper because before he left he gave me an extraordinary gift, a gift so precious that I will treasure it all my days, a gift that inspires me to write and make firm my thoughts.
And what was this gift? It was a love of poems and of learning to recite them by heart, taught not in a classroom by learned men but while walking in the hills and the valleys of Lancashire during long summer holidays.
And so I say to you, Reginald Jones, the man I walked down many a path with, and to whom I have a lot to be thankful for...
Thank you.

Look at this reminiscence and answer the questions below.

1 Reread paragraph 3. Turn the following words into their comparative and superlative form:

kind → ☐ → ☐

warm → ☐ → ☐

2 marks

2 Turn the words listed below into their comparative and superlative form.

tall   brave   thin   lazy

soft   large   wet   lucky

4 marks

3a **Word Focus:**
Find a word that means 'very special'.
Draw a line to show the two words which helped to create it.

☐

1 mark

3b **Word Focus:**
What is the comparative and superlative form of 'good'?
Comparative:
Superlative:
What do you notice?

3 marks

TOP CLASS - Vocabulary - Year 4

Suffixes

Add **er** or **est** to each root word.
Which is the comparative? Which is the superlative?
Investigate how we do this.
Write a rule to explain how we do this.
Are there any words that don't follow these rules?

Comparatives & Superlatives:

Rule 1:	Rule 2:	Rule 3:

Root Words:

tidy good big late small important wise early bad

weak beautiful sad large near clumsy wet expensive much

Rule 4:	Rule 5:	**Irregular:**

Homework
Write about somebody you have loved very much.
- When and where were they born?
- Who were their parents? Did they have siblings?
- Why do you treasure their friendship?
- How did they help you A] in the past and B] today?

Vocabulary

Revisit the text on page 29. Answer each question below.
Highlight the words you explore in the text itself.
Think of ways in which you can learn each one.
Can you act it out or draw it?
Does it remind you of a word you already know? Why?
How will you use your new words in the future?

Name: **Date:**

Which word means '**very special**'?	Which word means '**valuable**'?
Which two words help make this word?	Use this word in a sentence of your own.
What do you think the phrase '**make firm my thoughts**' means?	Is the word '**inspire**' positive or negative? (+) (−) What do you think it means?
What is a '**valley**'? Draw your answer.	What does the word '**stature**' suggest about the writer's granddad? ☐ He was tall ☐ He was short ☐ He had a good reputation ☐ He had a bad reputation
Why do you think the writer uses the term '**granddad**'?	In paragraph five, which word means '**to tell a story or poem from memory**'?

It is formal	It is informal
It is warm	It is cold
It is friendly	It is unfriendly

Shade your answers.   Check your answer in a dictionary.

Compound Words

Think about...
Join the following words to 'sun':
flower dial day set bathe tan
Add a word to begin each of these words:
proof fall mark hole melon fowl
What do we call these types of words?

Guided

Consider how and why people create compound words.

Why do you think people in the past created compound words to describe something that they had created? For example: the inventor of the first skateboard or the builder of the first lighthouse. Do you think this was a good or bad idea? Why? Why not? Can you think of any examples of your own?

Once done, answer the questions on page 33.

Independent

You are looking at ways in which compound words are created.

On your own, with a partner or in a small group; complete the task sheet provided to you by your teacher on page 34.

Once finished, cut off the homework task to help you broaden your word knowledge through practical reading within a variety of contexts.

Extension

Extend your personal vocabulary and understanding of specific words. Complete the task sheet on page 35.

If you have one, put any words you find interesting in your Personal Dictionary, together with an example of how it can be used effectively in a sentence.

*Answers available on the CD Rom.

Answers

1 bedcover, snowdrops, raincoats

2 footpath, nonetheless

3a Scouser

3b Mancunians, Glaswegians, Londoners, Geordies, Brummies
(It will be useful to have a map of the UK available so that each city can be located. Teachers may also wish to discuss place names which have appeared in the news or have been part of a recent topic)

Homework

- Arthur Wellesley (Duke of Wellington)
- 1817
- Calfskin leather
- Vulcanised rubber

Remember...
A **compound word** is created by joining two or more words together to create a new word.

Compound Words

A Path to Happiness

Small puddles littered the footpath and it was beginning to dawn on me that smart shoes and fresh jeans may not have been the wisest of decisions to make on a dreary Sunday morning. Nevertheless, throwing caution and common sense to the wind, I pressed on.

The carcass of a rabbit poked out from under a bedcover of ferns and a choir of snowdrops gathered to bow their heads in mournful respect. A family of red heads walked towards me. Wearing raincoats and wellingtons, even their spaniel looked satisfied.

'Good morning,' they chirped.

Behind them trailed two 'non-locals'. They too were dressed unseasonably: white trainers and heels a testament to their foolishness.

'Is it worth it?' I asked.

'Defo,' replied the Scouser.

I looked at his wife. She smiled sheepishly. She did not nod in agreement. Nor did she shake her head in disagreement. But her eyes (and mud spattered dress) told me that she did not quite agree.

As they passed by it began to drizzle. A dreary day was about to become even drearier. But I smiled, for I knew that as I walked down this muddy path, a fond memory was already beginning to forge.

Look at this anecdote and answer the questions below.

1 List the three compound words in paragraph two.

[   ]   [   ]   [   ]   3 marks

2 Find the two compound words in paragraph one.

Two word compound: [   ]   Three word compound: [   ]   2 marks

3a Word Focus: What do we call someone who comes from Liverpool?

[   ]   1 mark

3b Word Focus: What do we call people who come from the following cities?

Manchester   Glasgow   London

Newcastle   Birmingham

3 marks

Compound Words

A game for 2-4 players. Roll two dice. Multiply the two numbers together. If the answer is even choose a word beginning and colour it. If it is odd choose a word ending and colour it. When both parts of your compound word are the same colour, the word is yours. The player with the most compound words at the end of the game wins.

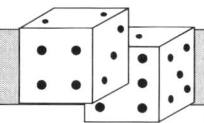

birth + day = birthday

Word beginnings:

finger	gold	birth	candle
basket	ear	skate	light
ship	sea	dragon	rattle
pop	straw	tomb	rain
wheel	week	play	grass

Word endings:

stone	fish	bow	ground
ball	snake	board	shore
fly	print	house	corn
end	stick	day	chair
hopper	berry	ache	wreck

Homework

Read about the Wellington boot.
- Who is this boot named after?
- In which year did they first appear?
- What material were the first made from?
- What are wellies usually made from today?

Vocabulary

Revisit the text on page 33. Answer each question below.
Highlight the words you explore in the text itself.
Think of ways in which you can learn each one.
Can you act it out or draw it?
Does it remind you of a word you already know? Why?
How will you use your new words in the future?

Name:　　　　　　　　　　　　**Date:**

Draw a footpath '**littered**' with small puddles.

Why might the author have chosen to use the word '**littered**'?

What colour clouds do you think of if they are described as being '**dreary**'?

Colour your answer.

Find a word for '**the dead body of an animal**'.

Draw and label your answer.

If you are a '**local**' where do you live?

☐ In the nearby area

☐ Outside of the nearby area

How do '**non-locals**' differ?

What does the phrase '**mud spattered**' mean?

Draw your answer.

Which part of the UK does a '**Scouser**' come from? Label it on the map.

Which word means '**to be unhappy and full of sadness**'?

Where are you likely to find a '**mourner**'?

Synonyms

Think about...
How might you describe a volcano?
Why is an eruption so awe inspiring?
Look at the following five words:
Irritated Cross Annoyed Furious Enraged
How are they similar? How are they different?

Guided

You have been given a poem to recite.

How will you make this poem (like the volcano itself) come alive? How will you use your voice to breathe life into the poet's words? Remember, to be an effective speaker, you must use your voice like a musical instrument. Like any great performer, your voice is a powerful tool. How will you read this poem? Will you speak fast or slow? When might you want to speed up or slow down?

Once done, answer the questions on page 37.

Independent

Consider how and why writers use synonyms and the effect a well-chosen synonym has on the reader.

On your own, with a partner or in a small group; complete the task sheet provided to you by your teacher on page 38.

Once finished, cut off the homework task to help you broaden your word knowledge through practical reading within a variety of contexts.

Extension

Extend your personal vocabulary and understanding of specific words. Complete the task sheet on page 39.

If you have one, put any words you find interesting in your Personal Dictionary, together with an example of how it can be used effectively in a sentence.

*Answers available on the CD Rom.

Answers

1 wrath, rage

2 grips
Allow for personal response.

3a thunderous

3b Like thunder, long and deep in sound you can hear it from afar.

Homework

- Italy (overlooking the Bay of Naples on the west coast)

- 24th August 79 AD

- Pompeii, Herculaneum

- Pyroclastic flow (red-hot gasses reaching temperatures of up to 600°C would have engulfed and killed fleeing inhabitants within seconds)

Remember...
A **synonym** is a word that has a similar meaning to another. However, there are no true synonyms in the English language. Every word has its own unique meaning. We must understand the shades of meaning a word has if we are to use it correctly and to its greatest effect.

Synonyms

PHOENIX RISING

The grumblings of Fire Mountain stop dead!
And for a moment…nothing
The earth trembles in expectation
And from his slumber the giant wakes
A burst of anger
A thunderous roar
Wrath unleashed
Rage untamed
Vengeful tongues lick the sky
A charmed cobra of smoke curls towards Heaven
Ash grips the air, choking the sky
We stand, captivated by fear and beauty, our eyes transfixed

PHOENIX RISING

Look at this poem and answer the questions below.

1 Find two strong synonyms the poet uses for 'anger'. How might you act each word out?

2 marks

2 Find a synonym the poet uses instead of 'holds'. How do these two words differ?

2 marks

3a Word Focus:
Find a word that means 'very loud'.

1 mark

3b Word Focus:
How else might you describe this word? Why?

3 marks

Synonyms

Look at these synonyms. Which describe a happy emotion? Which describe a sad emotion? Colour the positive words yellow and negative words blue. When you have found them all put each one in a sentence of your own. How strong would you describe each synonym? Why?

Word Search:

n	e	k	o	r	b	t	r	a	e	h	v	k	l
j	c	d	e	j	e	c	t	e	d	u	o	t	p
d	s	h	j	k	l	p	n	q	e	r	c	e	e
e	t	d	e	t	e	s	p	u	l	t	y	a	l
t	a	c	m	e	r	r	y	w	i	p	e	r	b
a	t	e	s	d	r	m	o	s	g	l	b	f	a
l	i	a	u	q	p	f	k	h	h	e	z	u	r
e	c	s	d	l	f	l	u	w	t	a	h	l	e
w	e	r	g	b	b	k	j	l	e	s	j	a	s
g	l	o	o	m	y	g	l	a	d	e	a	s	i
o	v	e	r	j	o	y	e	d	u	d	o	s	m

(−)
miserable
blue
hurt
tearful
heartbroken
dejected
gloomy
upset

(+)
ecstatic
delighted
elated
pleased
glad
merry
overjoyed
cheerful

Example: *The girl was upset because they had to leave early.*

 1 (2) 3 4 5 ☺

Homework

Read about the infamous eruption of Mt Vesuvius.
* Where is Mt Vesuvius?
* In which year did this volcano famously erupt?
* Which two Roman cities were destroyed?
* What killed the people of these cities?

Vocabulary

Revisit the text on page 37. Answer each question below.
Highlight the words you explore in the text itself.
Think of ways in which you can learn each one.
Can you act it out or draw it?
Does it remind you of a word you already know? Why?
How will you use your new words in the future?

Name: **Date:**

How would you describe a '**burst of anger**'?

expected   unexpected   fast

slow   sudden   gradual

Act it out.

How loud is a '**thunderous**' roar?

Quite loud   *Deafening*

   1   2   3   4   5

Write down the root of this word.
_____

Which word means '**sleep**'?

Z z z z z z z z z

Why do you think the earth '**trembles**' in the poem?

☐ Because it is cold

☐ Because it is frightened

☐ Because it is excited

Is the word '**grumbling**' positive or negative?

(+)   (−)

If you were grumbling, how would you be feeling?
_____

Which word tells us something or someone is '**wild**'?

Check your answer in a dictionary.

Find a family word that links with the idea of '**revenge**'.

Why do you think this?

Underline the root in the word **unleashed**

Draw the root word.
What do you think '**unleashed**' means?

TOP CLASS - Vocabulary - Year 4   39

Homophones

Think about...
Look at the following words:
**wood   tale   your   great   wheel
grate   would   we'll   tail   you're**
Which would you pair up? Why?
How is each word different in meaning?

Guided

You are reading a joke book. What do you think the punch line might be? Why?

Do lions like cooked vegetables? (No – they prefer them roar)
What's a librarian's favourite colour? (Read)
What did the ram write in his Valentine's Day card? (I love ewe)

Which joke did you like best? Why? How did the punch line make you laugh?

Once done, answer the questions on page 41.

Independent

Consider how some words that sound the same but are spelt differently possess different meanings.

On your own, with a partner or in a small group; complete the task sheet provided to you by your teacher on page 42.

Once finished, cut off the homework task to help you broaden your word knowledge through practical reading within a variety of contexts.

Extension

Extend your personal vocabulary and understanding of specific words. Complete the task sheet on page 43.

If you have one, put any words you find interesting in your Personal Dictionary, together with an example of how it can be used effectively in a sentence.

*Answers available on the CD Rom.

Answers

1 Weather: the condition above the Earth as in rain, wind or temperature. Whether: a conjunction used to introduce two or more possibilities.

2 There: [adverb] a place. Their: [determiner] belonging to them. They're: [informal contraction] short form of they are

3a mild

3b Food: not very strong in flavour, non-spicy. Person: gentle and calm, non-violent

Homework

- No specific answers are required for this homework. Finished books should be kept in their trays so that they can be shared during wet play times and favourite jokes displayed as part of a 'Joke of the Week'.

Instructions on how to make a book are on the CD Rom.

Remember...
A **homophone** is a word that sounds the same as another but is spelt differently and has a different meaning.

Homophones

Snow Joke

Leaves begin to carpet the forest floor. The villagers of the Little Big Horse tribe stand before their Chief and ask whether it will be cold or mild this coming winter.

Not knowing the answer, the Chief replies that it will indeed be cold and urges them to prepare by collecting enough wood to keep the tribe warm.

Being a good leader, he telephones the National Weather Service and asks the exact same question his people had asked him, to which comes the reply, "It is going to be a cold winter."

So the Chief gathers his people together and entreats them to collect more wood in order that they are really prepared for the coming winter.

A week goes by but still the north wind does not blow and snow has still not paid them a visit.

So he calls the National Weather Service again.

"It is going to be a very cold winter," is the reply.

So once again the Chief gathers his people together and implores them to collect every scrap of wood they can find so that they are fully prepared for such a harsh winter.

Two weeks go by. The Chief, still seeing no signs of winter, calls the National Weather Service for a third time. "Are you sure it is going to be cold this winter?"

"Absolutely, have you not seen the tribe of the Little Big Horse? They're collecting wood like there's no tomorrow!"

Look at the joke and answer the questions below.

1 Find the matching homophone. How are both words different?

Weather

2 marks

2 Find the matching homophones. How are the three words different?

There

3 marks

3a **Word Focus:**

Find a word that means 'not very cold'.

1 mark

3b **Word Focus:**

What does this same word mean when we use it to describe the following:

Food:

A person:

3 marks

TOP CLASS - Vocabulary - Year 4

Homophones

Match two homophones from the box below. Write each pair of words on a domino. Draw two different pictures on each domino to show what each different homophone means. Can you create some dominoes of your own?

Sounds Good to Me!

| Ireland | no | him | peace | poor | prey | sail | flower | rose | berry |
| bury | piece | know | island | rows | hymn | sale | pour | pray | flour |

Homework

Create your own mini joke book. Use the instructions your teacher gives you to make your mini book. Find some of your favourite jokes and put one on each page. Illustrate each joke to make your book colourful. Share your jokes with your friends.

Vocabulary

Revisit the text on page 41. Answer each question below.
Highlight the words you explore in the text itself.
Think of ways in which you can learn each one.
Can you act it out or draw it?
Does it remind you of a word you already know? Why?
How will you use your new words in the future?

Name: **Date:**

When would you describe winter as being '**harsh**'?	When would you describe winter as being '**mild**'?
Where would a '**tribe**' usually live? ☐ In a large city ☐ In a small town or village ☐ In the countryside ☐ In the wilderness	What do we often call the leader of such a group? Draw and label your answer.
If somebody asks the '**exact**' same question, what is special about it? ☐ Some words have been changed to make it easier to understand ☐ Not one word has been changed	Underline the root in the word **National** How does this differ from '**international**'?
Why does '**National Weather Service**' use capital letters?	Why does '**Little Big Horse**' use capital letters?

TOP CLASS - Vocabulary - Year 4

Homonyms

Think about...
Draw two pictures for each word:
box sink fish change
tie book spring match
What do we call these types of words?
What else do you notice? Which can you act out?

Guided

Get into groups of four. Practice reading the script. Act it out. Take turns playing the lead role of Mr Page (or Mrs Pages if you prefer).

How will you deliver your lines? Remember to act with your voice as well as your body. What voice will you choose? Consider your pitch, power, pace and volume.

Once done, answer the questions on page 45.

Independent

Consider how some words that are spelt the same and sound the same have more than one meaning.

On your own, with a partner or in a small group; complete the task sheet provided to you by your teacher on page 46.

Once finished, cut off the homework task to help you broaden your word knowledge through practical reading within a variety of contexts.

Extension

Extend your personal vocabulary and understanding of specific words. Complete the task sheet on page 47.

If you have one, put any words you find interesting in your Personal Dictionary, together with an example of how it can be used effectively in a sentence.

*Answers available on the CD Rom.

Answers

1 McGuire: tables
    Sanderson: trunks

2 rock [noun] a stone
           [noun] a type of music
    wave [noun] a line of water especially the sea
           [verb] a hand movement

3a fall [verb] UK – to fall over

3b trip [noun] a short journey there and back
            [verb] to lose your balance while walking or running

Homework

- Answers regarding the history of a school will often be found on a school's website. If so, give each learner a number of statements regarding your school. Ask each learner to visit the school website to discover which statements are 'True' and which are 'False'.

Remember...
A **homonym** is a word that sounds the same and is spelt the same as another but has a different meaning.

Homonyms

> Mr Page: No McGuire, when I asked you to learn your tables, I wasn't talking about you joining Mrs Turner's woodwork class.
> McGuire: Sorry, Sir.
> Mr Page: And no Sanderson, when Master Fischer spoke to you about not continuously forgetting your trunks, he was neither speaking about cutting down trees nor the plight of the African elephant.
> Sanderson: Sorry, Sir.
> Mr Page: And you Walker. When Mr Plane is trying to teach you about rock erosion and wave power, he isn't chatting to you about the decline in popularity of a certain genre of music or happy hand gestures.
> Walker: Sorry, Sir.
> Mr Page: And as for you Perkins...a school trip to see the American fall has nothing whatsoever to do with somebody going head over heels. [Sighs heavily and buries his head in his hands]
> Mr Page: Why do I even try? And before you ask, no I don't play rugby!

Look at this comedy sketch and answer the questions below.

1 Which homonym do the following characters get confused with? Why might this be?

McGuire: _____

Sanderson: _____

2 marks

2 Which two homonyms does Walker misunderstand? Why might this be?

I. _____

II. _____

2 marks

3a Word Focus:

Find the American word for 'autumn'.
Why might we find this word confusing?

1 mark

3b Word Focus:

Find a similar meaning word Mr Page uses.

Why might this homonym cause confusion?

3 marks

TOP CLASS - Vocabulary - Year 4

Homonyms

Choose a homonym from the list below.
Think of two meanings for each example.
Draw a picture in each circle, one for each meaning.
Is the word a verb or a noun?

It All Sounds The Same To Me!

bark

rock

sign

wave

sink

tie

fire

seal

park

stick

Homework
Read about the history of your own school.
- How did your school get its name?
- In which year was it built?
- What was the name of its first Head Teacher?
- How many pupils first attended the school?

Vocabulary

Revisit the text on page 45. Answer each question below.
Highlight the words you explore in the text itself.
Think of ways in which you can learn each one.
Can you act it out or draw it?
Does it remind you of a word you already know? Why?
How will you use your new words in the future?

Name: **Date:**

Write a definition for each homonym:

Tables: _____

Tables: _____

Write a definition for each homonym:

Fall: _____

Fall: _____

Write a definition for each homonym:

Trunks: _____

Trunks: _____

Trunks: _____

How much is a '**try**' worth in rugby?

Draw and label your answer.

Find a formal word that means '**to gradually become less**'.

What else can this word mean?
_____

Find a French word that means '**type**'.

Which word does Mr Page use that is related to the word '**continue**'?

Name three things that can cause rock '**erosion**'.

1. _____

2. _____

3. _____

TOP CLASS - Vocabulary - Year 4

Formal English

Think about...
You are invited on a school trip.
How formal will the invitation be?
How might it compare to the following:
An invite to the cinema   An invite to a wedding
What will be similar? What will be different?

Guided

A mysterious fair appears on the edge of town. But this is no ordinary fair. The people in charge are not who they appear to be. You climb on board the ghost train with your school friends oblivious to the dangers ahead!

What will happen next? After reading the extract, what questions are you left asking? Make a list with a partner. Share them with another pair. Who came up with the most interesting question? Why is it so good?

Once done, answer the questions on page 49.

Independent

You are considering the formality of words. Who would use them, where and when?

On your own, with a partner or in a small group; complete the task sheet provided to you by your teacher on page 50.

Once finished, cut off the homework task to help you broaden your word knowledge through practical reading within a variety of contexts.

Extension

Extend your personal vocabulary and understanding of specific words. Complete the task sheet on page 51.

If you have one, put any words you find interesting in your Personal Dictionary, together with an example of how it can be used effectively in a sentence.

*Answers available on the CD Rom.

Answers

1 Formal: deep, slow, monotone

2 Formal: remain, attempt, vacate
Informal: stay, try, leave

3a Nowt

3b Allow for personal response.

Homework

- Blackpool Pleasure Beach, UK
- 1930
- Joseph Emberton
- Cloggy

Remember...
We use **formal language** when we do not know the person we are talking to. It has a strong tone. We use it when what we are saying is important or the situation is serious.

Formal English

THE GHOST TRAIN

"All aboard," said the voice.

We clambered into the carriages giddy with excitement and waited for the silver bar to lock us in.

A large open mouth with plastic fangs gaped open before us and mechanical laughter echoed from deep inside. Two comical eyes turned from blood-red to sickly-green and we set off.

Fluorescent skeletons dangled above us and cardboard monsters shot out from behind polystyrene rocks and wooden gravestones. Wisps of smoke drifted through the air and cobwebs made of string clung to the ceiling. A blast of water attempted to scare us.

"Nowt scary about this," joked James and we all burst into laughter.

Suddenly, we jerked to a halt.

"Remain in your carriage," said the voice. "Do not attempt to vacate your carriage."

An amber light began to glow in the distance. Somehow we all knew that we weren't about to be rescued. Jennifer began to cry while Declan tried with all his might to lift the bar that was pinning us down. It was only then that he noticed the writing on the bar itself…

PRISONER TRANSPORT CARRIAGE - RESISTANCE IS FUTILE

Look at this extract from an adventure story and answer the questions below.

1 How do you think the voice speaks? Why? Act it out.

The voice: ☐ Formal   ☐ Informal

☐ High   ☐ Deep   ☐ Fast   ☐ Slow   ☐ Monotone

4 marks

2 Find three formal words in paragraph seven. How might you say each word informally?

Formal:

Informal:

3 marks

3a Word Focus:

Find an informal word James uses that means 'nothing'.

1 mark

3b Word Focus:

What do you think the writing on the silver bar means?

3 marks

TOP CLASS - Vocabulary - Year 4

Formal English

Look at each illustrated sign.
Colour the formal words in red.
Then match each sign with its informal partner.
Colour the informal words green.
Where might you see each sign?
Why do you think that?

What Do You Notice?

(a) Smoking is prohibited in this building.	(b) Should you require any further assistance telephone: 0800 678876	○ Lost! Our much loved puppy Benny. If found, call 07835 2762861	○ Please check your change. Mistakes can't be sorted out after.
(c) **Do not** lean your bicycle on this window. It is incredibly annoying!	(d) PERMITS CAN BE PURCHASED FROM THE FISHING LODGE 9AM – 5PM	○ In the event of a fire, leave the building straight away.	○ Skateboards aren't allowed in this area.
(e) Skateboards are not permitted in this area.	(f) In the event of a fire, vacate the building immediately.	○ Smoking is banned in this building.	○ Permits can be bought from the Fishing Lodge 9am – 5pm
(g) Please examine your change. Mistakes cannot be rectified afterwards.	(h) Missing! Our much loved puppy Benjamin. If located, telephone 07835 2762861	○ If you need any more help, phone: **0800 678876**	○ Don't lean your bike on this window. It's really annoying!

Homework

Read about the world's first Ghost Train.
- Where was the first Ghost Train ever ridden?
- In which year did this ride open?
- Who designed it?
- Who supposedly haunts this ride today?

Vocabulary

Revisit the text on page 49. Answer each question below.
Highlight the words you explore in the text itself.
Think of ways in which you can learn each one.
Can you act it out or draw it?
Does it remind you of a word you already know? Why?
How will you use your new words in the future?

Name: **Date:**

How would describe a '**blast**' of air or water?

Fast	Slow
Strong	Weak
Pleasant	Unpleasant

Shade your answers.

Find a word that describes '**a very bright colour that can be seen in the dark**'.

Find an example of this in your classroom.

Which of the following traffic lights would you describe as being '**amber**'?

Colour in your answer.

If you are '**giddy**' how are you feeling?

happy   unhappy   bored   excited

How are you acting?

silly   serious

Find a formal word that means to '**leave**'.

Why do you think the voice uses this word instead of '**leave**'?

Find the informal word James uses that means '**nothing**'.

What might this suggest about James?

Find a synonym the writer uses instead of '**climbed**'.

Which synonym do you think is faster and more fun?

If you '**jerked to a halt**', how would you stop?

Quickly	Suddenly
With force	Gently

Act it out.

TOP CLASS - Vocabulary - Year 4

Informal Speech

Think about...
Look at these informal names:
Sam Nat Chris Nicky Danny
Rewrite each name formally.
Which is male? Which is female?
How would you shorten your classmates' names?

Guided

Revisit the sign Mrs Wang and Chloe make in the text. Why do you think they chose to write it in this style? Do you think the message would have been stronger if it had been written formally? Why? Why not? Which style do you prefer? Why? Why might it be necessary to write a sign formally, even if you do not like writing in this style?

Once done, answer the questions on page 53.

Independent

Consider how and why we use informal language, when it is appropriate and when it is not.

On your own, with a partner or in a small group; complete the task sheet provided to you by your teacher on page 54.

Once finished, cut off the homework task to help you broaden your word knowledge through practical reading within a variety of contexts.

Extension

Extend your personal vocabulary and understanding of specific words. Complete the task sheet on page 55.

If you have one, put any words you find interesting in your Personal Dictionary, together with an example of how it can be used effectively in a sentence.

*Answers available on the CD Rom.

Answers

1 Informal

2 I. Life's – Life is
II. That's – That is

3a Present: [noun] a gift, [tense] now

3b Allow for personal response.

Homework

- 1952, 1964, 1976, 1988, 2000, 2012, 2024, 2036 (a twelve year cycle)

- Confident and hardworking. Full of energy and determination they will inspire people. Don't like routine and are excited by new projects. Show loyalty to friends, are popular and fun-loving.

- Allow for personal response.

Remember...
We use informal language when we write to our friends or family because it is warm and friendly. Often what we are writing is heartfelt. However, if we do not know the person or what we are talking about is serious, then we must use **formal language** instead.

Informal Speech

THE PAPER DRAGON

A scrunched up ball of paper sat at the bottom of the basket and the gold crayon, bought especially for the task, lay discarded on the desk beyond.

Try as she might, Chloe Flynn could not put down on paper what she had already drawn in her head.

Determined to create a masterpiece, she had battled all afternoon to get it just right. Yet despite her many attempts and countless rubbings out, she had finally admitted defeat. Disposing of her failure she had quietly gone to bed. A fire-breathing worm with wings was simply not good enough to adorn the front of Mrs Wang's Get Well Soon card. Another plan would need to be dreamt up.

Mrs Wang was the owner of The Old Curiosity Shop on Jubilee Road. She was also the kindest and wisest woman that Chloe knew. Her command of the English language was not the greatest but her warm smile and loving deeds rang out far beyond the village and all that came across her loved her very much.

It was Chloe that had helped write and decorate the sign for her shop window not long after she had left the children's ward for her final treatment, a sign that told you more about the owner than the shop itself.

Life's a gift
That's why we call it 'The Present'

The clock struck twelve. The basket began to move.

Read the opening of this magical tale and answer the questions below.

1 Is the sign in Mrs Wang's shop window formal or informal?

☐ Formal   ☐ Informal

1 mark

2 Find two examples in the sign that evidence this. Write each example formally.

I. _____

II. _____

2 marks

3a Word Focus:

Which word in the sign is a homonym?

1 mark

3b Word Focus:

What do you think the sign means?

3 marks

Informal Speech

What we say is often different to what we write down.
Match an informal speech bubble with a formal note.
Colour the informal words yellow.
Colour the formal words purple.
Can you think of an example of your own?

Say What?

Informal speech bubbles:
- Please don't worry. It'll all be OK.
- It's killin' me!
- Cheers mate.
- I'm shattered. I'm off for a kip.
- Can you fix my bike? It's got a flat tyre.
- Call the cops; some toe rag's nicked my wallet!
- That's stupid!
- If you chuck litter, you'll be fined two hundred quid.
- He failed the exam? I bet he's gutted.
- You what?
- I'm dying for the loo, Miss.

Formal notes:
- That is ridiculous!
- I beg your pardon.
- Is it possible for you to repair my bicycle? It has a puncture.
- If you drop litter, you will be fined £200.
- I am extremely tired. I am going to have a sleep.
- May I go to the toilet, Mrs Mullighan?
- Thank you my good friend.
- Telephone the police, some scoundrel has stolen my wallet!
- He failed his examination? I expect he is terribly upset.
- Please do not worry. Everything will be fine.
- It is incredibly painful.

Homework

Read about the Chinese dragon.
- What is the Chinese symbol for the dragon?
- Were you born in the year of the dragon?
- If yes - what qualities are you supposed to have?
- If not - what is your Chinese zodiac sign?

Vocabulary

Revisit the text on page 53. Answer each question below.
Highlight the words you explore in the text itself.
Think of ways in which you can learn each one.
Can you act it out or draw it?
Does it remind you of a word you already know? Why?
How will you use your new words in the future?

Name: **Date:**

Which word in the shop's name means **'to have a strong wish to know or learn about something'**?

Which word describes **'a work of art that is made with great skill'**?

How is this compound word made?

Which word means **'to be left to one side because you no longer need it'**?

Which word is a formal word that means **'throwing away'** or **'getting rid'** of something?

Create a **'scrunched up'** ball using scrap paper. What does it tell us about the paper itself?

If a person **'scrunched up'** a piece of work, how are they likely to be feeling?

Act it out.

How likely is a person to succeed if they are **'determined'**?

Unlikely   Likely

1   2   3   4   5

Why?

Which word means **'to add something decorative to make something look more beautiful'**?

TOP CLASS - Vocabulary - Year 4

Similes

Think about...
Look at an eagle in flight.
How might you describe it?
Write out your sentence and share it.
Did you use 'like' or 'as' in your work?
What affect does this have on the reader?

Guided

You are considering how and why writers choose to use (or avoid using) similes.

What is a simile? Why do you think some writers use them to describe something? Revisit some of the similes your classmates used to describe an eagle. What happens to the sentence if you remove the simile? What do we call this new kind of kind of description? Why do you think some writers prefer this to using similes?

Once done, answer the questions on page 57.

Independent

You are looking at ways in which similes are created and what effect this has on the reader.

On your own, with a partner or in a small group; complete the task sheet provided to you by your teacher on page 58.

Once finished, cut off the homework task to help you broaden your word knowledge through practical reading within a variety of contexts.

Extension

Extend your personal vocabulary and understanding of specific words. Complete the task sheet on page 59.

If you have one, put any words you find interesting in your Personal Dictionary, together with an example of how it can be used effectively in a sentence.

*Answers available on the CD Rom.

Answers

1 As happy as larks – calm, contented and very happy

2 As bald as a coot
As dead as a dodo
As proud as a peacock
As sick as a parrot

3a incision

3b stuff
Informal style = relaxed, more appealing to children (their target audience)

Homework

- The Royal Society for the Protection of Birds

- 3rd November, 1904

- Avocet (1955)

- 1989

Remember...
A **simile** compares one thing to another. It often uses the words '**like**' or '**as**' when doing so. For example:
She flew out of the door like a bat out of Hell.
He stormed into class with a face like thunder.

Similes

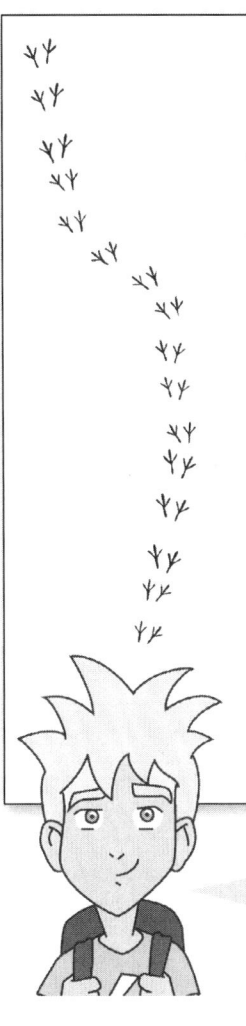

Make a Speedy Bird Cake

Make this quick and easy cake and keep our feathered friends as happy as larks this winter.

Stuff you will need:
Good quality bird seed, raisins, unsalted peanuts, suet or lard, clean yoghurt pots, string, a sturdy mixing bowl and a pair of scissors.

What to do:
1. Carefully make a small incision in the bottom of your yoghurt pot. Thread a piece of string through the hole and tie a knot on the inside. Leave enough string so that you can secure the pot to a tree branch or a bird table.
2. Allow the lard to warm slightly to room temperature, but don't melt it. Leaving it out of the fridge overnight is your best option. Then cut it up into small cubes and put into the mixing bowl.
3. Add the other ingredients to the bowl and mix them together with your fingertips. Keep adding the seed/raisins/peanuts to the mixture and squidging it until the fat holds it all together.
4. Fill your yoghurt pots with the bird cake mixture and put them in the fridge to set. After an hour or so, each pot will be firm enough for you to hang outside in the garden.

Look at the set of instructions and answer the questions below.

1 What simile is used in the introduction? Why might it have been chosen?

_____

_____

2 marks

2 Match the two parts of each well-known simile.

As bald as	As dead as	As proud as	As sick as
a parrot	a peacock	a dodo	a coot

4 marks

3a **Word Focus:**
Find a formal word for 'cut'.

1 mark

3b **Word Focus:**
Which informal word does the writer use instead of 'equipment'?

Why do you think this word was chosen?

3 marks

TOP CLASS - Vocabulary - Year 4

Similes

Read the beginnings of some well-known similes. Match them to their correct ending and draw a picture to help you remember it. When done, put your simile into a sentence. Create two new similes of your own too.

Similes:

As bold as ✓	As pure as	As clean as
As dull as	As sturdy as	As pretty as
As snug as	As sweet as	As steady as
As black as	Like father,	As silent as

a picture	pitch	the grave
dishwater	honey	a whistle
brass ✓	a rock	the driven snow
a bug in a rug	an oak	like son

Example: *She didn't care; <u>as bold as brass</u> she stormed into the classroom and slammed the door shut.*

Homework

Read about the RSPB. Official website: *www.rspb.org.uk*
- What does the acronym RSPB stand for?
- When was this acronym adopted?
- Which bird was chosen as its symbol? When?
- When did the RSPB celebrate its centenary?

Vocabulary

Revisit the text on page 57. Answer each question below.
Highlight the words you explore in the text itself.
Think of ways in which you can learn each one.
Can you act it out or draw it?
Does it remind you of a word you already know? Why?
How will you use your new words in the future?

Name: **Date:**

Which word does the writer use instead of '**equipment**'?

_____

How formal is this word?

Very informal   *Very formal*

1   2   3   4   5

Find the formal word '**incision**'.
What does it tell us?

☐ The blade is very sharp
☐ The blade is not very sharp
☐ The cut is made slowly with great care
☐ The cut is made quickly with no thought

What does the adjective '**sturdy**' tell us about the mixing bowl?

☐ It is strong
☐ It is delicate

What does it suggest about how we mix?

If something is '**firm**', how hard is it?

Very soft   *Very hard*

1   2   3   4   5

Which word, in the same paragraph, links with this idea?

Find a word that is related to the word '**security**'.

What do you think it means?

Find a synonym the writer uses for '**choice**'.

Is this word formal or informal?

Can you spot the nonsense word in this text?

What do you think it means? Act it out.

Find an adjective that simply means '**fast**'.

Underline the root word in your answer.

TOP CLASS - Vocabulary - Year 4   59

Creative Word Play

Think about...
Look at a map of the UK.
Where is London?
Look at a map of London.
Where is the East End?
What do we call people who come from this area?

Guided

You are learning about the origins of Cockney Rhyming Slang.

Have you heard of this term before? If so, can you give an example? If not, what do you think it could be? Listen to some examples. Can you work out what is happening? How might you learn Cockney Rhyming Slang if you are not from this part of the world?

Once done, answer the questions on page 61.

Independent

You overhear two Cockneys having a chat. Can you work out what they are really saying?

On your own, with a partner or in a small group; complete the task sheet provided to you by your teacher on page 62.

Once finished, cut off the homework task to help you broaden your word knowledge through practical reading within a variety of contexts.

Extension

Extend your personal vocabulary and understanding of specific words. Complete the task sheet on page 63.

If you have one, put any words you find interesting in your Personal Dictionary, together with an example of how it can be used effectively in a sentence.

*Answers available on the CD Rom.

Answers

1
- Phone: dog and bone
- Stairs: apples and pears
- A thief: tea leaf
- A lie: pork pie

2
- Daisy roots: boots
- Whistle & flute: suit
- Loaf of bread: head
- Ruby Murray: curry

3a Adam and Eve: believe

3b Bob (or Bobby) is the short form of Robert. Robert Peel created the modern police force.

Homework

- 19th February 1985 (BBC1)
- Julia Smith, Tony Holland
- Walford (East End of London), Albert Square
- Prince Albert (husband to Queen Victoria)

Remember...
Cockney rhyming slang was created in the East End of London. It is very informal and is usually spoken not written. It replaces certain words with special rhymes or phrases. For example: He went up the apples and pears (stairs) or let's go for a Ruby Murray (curry).

Creative Word Play

Would You Adam and Eve It?

Cockney rhyming slang can be traced back to the early part of the nineteenth century, when in 1824 Sir Robert Peel formed the first official police force stationed at Bow Street, London.

Known locally as the Bow Street Runners or Peelers, today we often use the more affectionate and informal term Bobbies (Bob being the short form of Robert). Whatever they were called, they soon gained a fearsome reputation for solving crime.

Criminal gangs and petty thieves alike were worried that they would be heard planning their next crime or boasting about the one they had just committed. So instead they began to create a secret code that they hoped the police would not understand. And would you Adam and Eve it, Cockney rhyming slang was born.

Cockney Slang is a coded language that uses a phrase that rhymes with a word rather than the word itself. Thus 'stairs' becomes 'apples and pears', 'phone' becomes 'dog and bone' and 'thief' becomes 'tea leaf'.

And if you really want to conceal what you are saying, then you can do so by dropping the rhyming part of the word altogether. 'Have a butchers at this' (butcher's hook = look) and 'stop telling me porkies' (pork pies = lies) are two great examples.

Look at the museum leaflet and answer the questions below.

1 What would a Cockney call the following?

A phone: _____ Stairs: _____

A thief: _____ A lie: _____

4 marks

2 What would a Cockney call the following? Use the Internet to help you.

A pair of boots: _____ A suit: _____

Your head: _____ A curry: _____

4 marks

3a Word Focus:
The title uses Cockney Rhyming Slang. What do you think it means?

1 mark

3b Word Focus:
Why do people in the UK call the police 'bobbies'?

3 marks

Creative Word Play

Read each sentence out loud in a Cockney accent. Underline the Cockney Rhyming Slang in each one. Draw and label a picture for each answer.

Cockney Rhyming Slang:

1. daisy roots (boots)	2.	3.	4.	5.

1. Put your <u>daisy roots</u> on, the path is too muddy for trainers.
2. Use your loaf of bread, it can't be that difficult.
3. Dad put on his best whistle and flute for the wedding.
4. Don't say a Dickey Bird to anyone, it's a surprise.
5. Have you any bread and honey? I've forgotten my wallet.
6. Will someone answer that dog and bone? I'm busy.
7. Fancy a Ruby Murray tonight? I'm starving.
8. Shut your north and south and get over here.
9. I'd love a nice hot cup of Rosy Lee, thanks.
10. Is that his real hair or a syrup of fig?

6.	7.	8.	9.	10.

Homework

Read about the TV series EastEnders.
- When was the first episode broadcast?
- Who created it?
- Where is this soap opera set?
- Who is this square named after?

Vocabulary

Revisit the text on page 61. Answer each question below.
Highlight the words you explore in the text itself.
Think of ways in which you can learn each one.
Can you act it out or draw it?
Does it remind you of a word you already know? Why?
How will you use your new words in the future?

Name: **Date:**

Find a word in the final paragraph that means '**to hide**'.

_____

Is this word formal or informal?

☐ Formal   ☐ Informal

Underline the root in the word

stationed

What do you think this word means?

_____
_____
_____

How formal is '**slang**'?

Very Informal   *Very Formal*

(1   2   3   4   5)

Can you think of an example of your own?

_____

If a Cockney called you a '**tea leaf**', what would they be calling you?

_____
_____
_____

What do you think '**petty thieves**' steal?

☐ Very expensive things
☐ Inexpensive things
☐ Rare objects
☐ Common, everyday objects

Find another word in the opening paragraph that means '**to be made or created**'.

[   ]

Who created what?

Find the word '**affectionate**'.
What do you think it means?

☐ Loving
☐ Unloving

Check your answer in a dictionary.

If a person is '**boasting**', what are they doing?

_____

Is this positive or negative?

Negative   *Positive*

(1   2   3   4   5)

TOP CLASS - Vocabulary - Year 4

Notes: